YVONNE PORCELLA
Magical
Four-Patch and Nine-Patch Quilts

C&T PUBLISHING

© 2001 Yvonne Porcella

Editor: Beate Marie Nellemann

Technical Editors: Sara Kate MacFarland and Lynn Koolish

Copy Editor: Stacy Chamness

Cover Designer: Christina D. Jarumay

Design Director/Book Designer: Christina D. Jarumay

Illustrator: Kandy Petersen

Photography: Sharon Risedorph unless otherwise noted

Production Assistants: Kirstie McCormick and Tim Manibusan

Published by C & T Publishing, Inc., P.O. Box 1456, Lafayette, California 94549

Attention Teachers: C & T Publishing, Inc. encourages you to use this book as a text for teaching. Contact us at 800-284-1114 or www.ctpub.com for more information about the C&T Teachers Program.

Library of Congress Cataloging-in-Publication Data

Porcella, Yvonne.

  Magical four-patch and nine-patch quilts / Yvonne Porcella.

    p. cm.

  ISBN 1-57120-157-2

  1. Patchwork–Patterns. 2. Quilting–Patterns. I. Title.

  TT835 .P645 2001

  746.46'041–dc21

                                                2001002590

Printed in Hong Kong

10 9 8 7 6 5 4 3 2 1

Table of Contents

To all the quilt makers who are inspired
to try something different.

Acknowledgments

To my husband Bob, who knows more about computers than I do, and is
a willing companion, friend, and partner in all our life experiences.
Thanks to Nancy Podolsky and Cathie I. Hoover, who each graciously
volunteered to make a sample quilt for this book. With the very basic
information of my numbering system they made such beautiful quilts.
My good friend, Kay Elson, lent her nimble fingers to hand quilt one
project, and she is always so agreeable to help when needed. To Paula
Reid I say thanks for teaching me that "yes", I can turn one of my quilt
tops over to an expert to have it machine quilted. Judy Mullen has the
best fabric stash and extraordinary talents. I am grateful to her for shar-
ing her collection of the 1930s reproduction fabrics and making the
blocks.

Introduction

I have never made a large quilt using a traditional repeat block format. Not because I do not respect the efforts involved, but because I do not like the precision required to measure and calculate fabrics to make a large quilt. This book shares the way I put together Four-Patch and Nine-Patch blocks to make interesting quilts that do not have a repeat block sequence.

I thought you might enjoy seeing my first attempt to make a traditional Nine-Patch quilt. My color selection was red and white. I made five perfect Nine-Patch blocks all alike with red corners and center. I did not know how to calculate what the sewn block would measure, nor did I trust my ability to make all five blocks the same size. I waited until these were stitched, and then I cut four plain white blocks to match the size of my Nine-Patch blocks. I sewed three rows together, the top and bottom rows had a Nine-Patch block on each end with the white square in the middle, and the other row had white squares on the ends and one Nine-Patch block between.

I was so happy when I saw the results, a perfect 13 1/2" x 13 1/2" larger Nine-Patch block made from five smaller Nine-Patches and four squares. I loved the way the red small squares made a diagonal line across the quilt from corner to corner. In fact, I turned the block every which way, and it always looked great. Suddenly it dawned on me that if I made more of these blocks I would have a very big quilt to dazzle my family. I entertained that idea for about a minute until I realized that I would have to hand quilt the large quilt. Since I was a novice to quilting, my mind struggled to imagine how much time it would take me to complete a big quilt. When I was young, my mother had said, "It takes a lifetime to make a quilt," and I believed her! She was

probably talking about the quilting stitches because I had pieced my Nine-Patch block together in record time. Upon looking at my one block, I reasoned that it was just as beautiful in a small size. I quilted it with a diagonal grid pattern and stitched a red with gold polka dot binding around the edges. So ends my story of making a traditional quilt. Again, it is not because I don't love them; it is a matter of what comes easy for me.

Some years later, upon the occasion of the impending birth of a second grandchild, I selected a Nine-Patch as the pattern to make a baby quilt. Using a limited number of blocks alternating with a plain fabric block, and adding a wide border fabric, the quilt was done by the deadline. The fifteen blocks each feature three colors, seven blocks have a twin color block and number fifteen is special. When I unfurled my quilt at the baby shower, the guests gasped. Someone said, "That's a baby quilt? Isn't **that** colorful!!"

My first quilt; *Red and White Nine-Patch block,* **13 1/2" x 13 1/2"**

Quilt for Vincent Timothy, 45" x 65", Yvonne Porcella

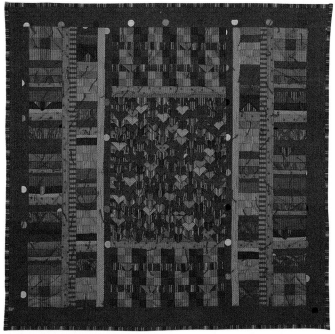

Carro 648, 46" x 46", Yvonne Porcella

When I cut the white blocks for the first quilt to match the size of my red-and-white pieced Nine-Patch blocks, I hit upon a method that for me has been a part of all future aspects of my quilting, as well as wearable art. I only measure what I have to, and I never calculate what a finished block should be before I begin. I sew the Four-Patch or Nine-Patch block using the strip piecing method. The strip widths are measured when cut, and each block has four or nine strips all the same width. The strips are stitched together, and after the final pressing I measure the block. If the Nine-Patch is to be sewn to a Four-Patch, I add additional strips of fabric to the smaller block, and then join it to a larger block. Using more strips of fabric, I piece together all the sewn blocks adding strips of color to enlarge the blocks where needed. Color choices and placement of these strips gives spark to the blocks. Before too long, a collection of blocks becomes a quilt. The sizes of the quilt depends on how many blocks I have and to what extent I add additional strips.

In *Carro 648*, the quilt began with the idea to make a whole quilt using folded prairie points. After making a small sample and spending way too much time ironing prairie points, I decided to add Four-Patch and Nine-Patch blocks and strips to surround the sample. The quilt length grew from the center by stitching Four-Patch alternating color blocks together to make horizontal rows with striped fabric sashing to extend the top and bottom of the center Prairie Point block. Then vertical rows of Nine-Patch blocks and strips were added to increase the width. The construction is similar to the *Plaids and Stripes* pattern on page 29.

In another quilt, *Mother's Day at the Zoo*, Four-Patch and Nine-Patch blocks were sewn together to make rows and large squares or rectangles. The blocks were made using just two colors, and when joined in rectangles or large squares they formed a checkerboard pattern. This quilt features specialty fabrics, and the pattern is similar to the *Sun and Sky* quilt on page 32.

As you can see, there is a big leap in design from my red and white Nine-Patch square (on page 5) to the quilts you see in this book. I wanted to share with you the system I used to make these original and colorful quilts. When you try my "Magical Numbering" system with a limited number of colors, you will make a new quilt, reflecting your personal colors and placement of the blocks and sashing.

Mother's Day at the Zoo, 55" x 77 $^1/_2$", Yvonne Porcella

Detail from *Mother's Day at the Zoo*

one

The Numbering System

The projects in this book are based on my "Magical Numbering" system. Most quilts use eleven fabrics and the block patterns are simple Four-Patch and Nine-Patch. When you look at each project, you'll see what color choices I made and how the color combinations worked in the blocks and sashing.

When I start to make a quilt using this numbering system, I lay out my fabrics, putting my contrast colors in the 4 and 5 positions. While I don't have any specific formula for ordering the fabrics, I look at my standard block number combinations (see page 9) and think about what colors will be next to each other in the blocks. I want to make sure I like the combinations and there will be enough contrast between the colors.

I number the fabrics from 1 to 11. Then, using my standard block number combinations, I cut out squares of the fabrics and make paste-ups of the blocks. I look at the blocks and evaluate them—do they have enough contrast or are the colors too close to each other? Would I rather use just two colors in a Nine-Patch instead of three colors? Will I want to use all of the standard block combinations or will I want to use fewer combinations or perhaps, even more?

If I don't like the way the colors are working in the blocks, I rearrange the order of the fabrics in my chart and make new paste-ups of the colors in the blocks using my standard block number combinations.

When I'm happy with my blocks, I cut strips and sew the blocks. I also cut strips of all the colors to use for sashing. From a central starting point, I lay out one or two blocks and a few sashing pieces and see what emerges. Then I take a step back and look to see what blocks and sashing I want to use next.

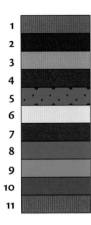

Numbering system

I am always aware of contrast, so when I place colors in the numbering sequence, I always reserve a few colors to use as accent strips as I assemble the quilt top. As you construct the quilt, the motto to keep in mind is: "when in doubt, use the two accent fabrics."

You'll need to select eleven fabrics in prints or solids.

■ Choose a color theme and select three fabrics that are variations of that theme color—such as three prints in small, medium, and large scale in this color, or three values or three textures of it.

■ Select two different shades of a second color.

■ Select two different textures—for instance chintz or satin weave—of a third color.

■ Select two values of a fourth color.

■ Finally select two other colors to act as contrast, usually Fabric 4 and 5.

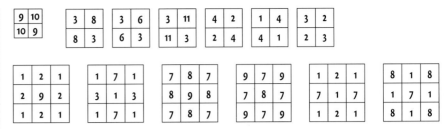

Standard block number combinations

Example of color combination for the small Four-Patch Block A

Large Four-Patch blocks—two fabric combinations for each Four-Patch block.

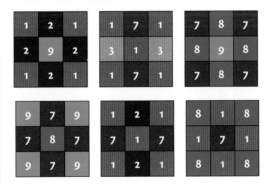

Example of color combinations for the large Four-Patch block

Nine-Patch blocks—three different fabrics for each Nine-Patch block.

Example of color combinations for the Nine-Patch block

The reason I start with this system is that with suitable numbering of the fabrics, I know that I will get variety and movement within the quilt while the repetition of colors provides continuity and balance. I limit the number of colors I use in the blocks so the other colors used in the sashing will provide interest and contrast. Of course, I always feel free to break "my rules" when inspiration strikes, but I've found that my numbering system always gives me a good starting point.

The projects in this book will give you the specifics you need to make quilts similar to the ones shown. However, I sincerely hope that you will feel adventurous and try out your own colors and combinations. Look at the different block combinations used in the projects for a good idea of the variety of the possibilities.

TWO

General Instructions

My design approach to a quilt is to cut strips of all the fabrics I have selected for a project and lay them out as described in the previous chapter on The Numbering System. I number the fabrics and make paste-ups of the blocks. I look at how the colors interact and I rearrange the fabrics as necessary and make new paste-ups until I'm happy with the blocks. When the blocks are done, I begin the process of designing the quilt top. The way I put the blocks together and add sashing is what makes each of my quilts different. I use strip piecing to add to the size of each block. The cut strips are also used to join blocks together. This method requires only cutting the original strips accurately and adding more strips to the quilt top until the desired size is reached. My motto is "if it isn't big enough, just add a strip." This method also allows for a very personal quilt design, since two people could choose the same colors, prints, and blocks, but sew them together differently. Two good examples of this are the quilts by the guest artists (see page 45).

CUTTING THE STRIPS

If you are using a 40" wide fabric, the best way to cut it is to double up the folded fabric to 20", and fold it again to 10". Then cut with a rotary cutter and plastic ruler. I usually cut my strips into 1", 1 $1/2$", and 2" widths. You may need to cut some wider strips for some projects. When cutting your strips it is important to cut them accurately so that when you add them to your blocks they will match up correctly.

In the diagrams that show the construction sequence, I give you the cut width of the strips that I used. You just need to measure the length of the unit you are adding onto to determine the length of the strips.

Please note that all given measurements include a $1/4$" seam allowance.

MAKING A FOUR-PATCH BLOCK

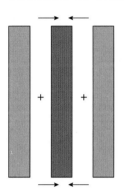

Sew two same width strips together.
Press towards the darker side.

Cut strips into units the same width as the original strip.

Example: If the strips you are using are 1 1/2" wide, cut the sewn strips into units that are 1 1/2" wide.

Sew units together.

MAKING A NINE-PATCH BLOCK

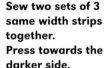

**Sew two sets of 3 same width strips together.
Press towards the darker side.**

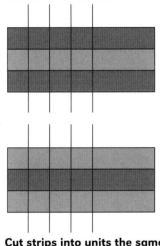

Cut strips into units the same width as the original strip.

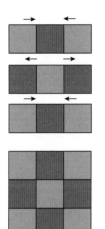

Sew units together.

SETTING THE BLOCKS

Most quilts can be identified as a diagonal set or straight set. These terms refer to how the blocks are placed and joined together.

A **diagonal set** begins with a 45° angle, and the rows of joined blocks are set along the angle line.

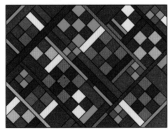

Straight set identifies the blocks set horizontally and vertically at right angles to each other.

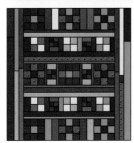

I begin my quilt top with one block and add strips of fabric. I continue to add strips to selected sides of my block until I have joined several blocks together. This becomes the **Center Unit.** If I want to add a "bar" to any side of my original Center Unit, I cut a strip the length of the side and add this to the Center Unit. This **Pieced Unit** can be any length or width and can be composed of blocks and/or strips of different fabrics. The bars around the extended Center Unit are added without worrying about the sizes on each of the four sides—a 3" wide Pieced Unit can be stitched on one edge of the center and a 7" wide Pieced Unit can be stitched to the other edge. In my finished quilts, even I cannot determine my starting point without careful examination.

DEFINING THE QUILT SIZE

Because my strip-piecing method develops one unit at a time, I establish my quilt size goal by cutting a piece of muslin the proposed finished size of my quilt. I use this as a guide to how much piecing I must construct to cover the desired area. I prefer to place this foundation fabric on my worktable for a small quilt, or on the floor or design wall for a large quilt. As the construction of my Pieced Units develop, I lay out what I have on the foundation and look at where I want the next accent color or block to appear. When you look at the projects in this book, notice the accent colors, and how and where the blocks are placed.

These are not random accidents, but rather a carefully thought-out plan that grows as I continuously look at how the quilt top is developing. For me, this is the creative part of the project, and I often stare at the developing design and let my eyes wander over the surface until I make a judgment on where the next color or block should go.

STRIP PIECING

When using the strip-piecing method of construction for the quilt top, a diagonal setting may require a bit more "fill-in" on the four areas that form the outer corner edges of the design. In my method, the large center area of the quilt top is composed by constantly enlarging the Center Unit. The challenge comes when reaching the four corner edges. These areas of the quilt require sewing a group of blocks and strips together to fill the shape that forms the corners. Sew these to the Center Unit and trim the edges to fit.

FLIP AND STITCH

For a small project, you may want to sew the blocks and Pieced Units directly onto the foundation. *Apron Strings* (page 37) was made this way. The first block or Center Unit is pinned to the foundation fabric, either in the middle or near the edge, in a straight or diagonal setting. The second strip or Pieced Unit is pinned with right sides together over the first strip or block. Sew along the pinned edge with a 1/4" seam allowance. Remove the pins and turn the Fabric 2 strip so it is right side up, press it flat with a steam iron. Continue sewing strips and Pieced Units around the Center Unit, pressing after each sewing until the foundation backing is covered with patchwork.

MAKING A LARGER QUILT

Some of the quilt patterns are for small quilts. To enlarge any of these patterns you can double or triple the number of blocks and strips, or use wider strips to make the blocks. The design principle works the same; just continue adding blocks and Pieced Units until you reach the desired size.

This book will help you make a quilt, teach you a process to break away from a repeating block style or measured pattern quilt, and to use strip-piecing with simple measurements to make very special and personal quilts.

A FEW SUGGESTIONS ON COLOR

I have never seen a color I don't like, which makes selecting colors an easy process. When I made my first quilts, I collected new cotton fabrics. At the time, my fabric collection only included my own hand-woven fabrics or cotton fabrics from other countries. Before I could begin to do patchwork, I had to acquire 100% cotton fabrics. My first major purchase was one yard cuts of 150 solid colors. I ordered these from a mail-order company, and for me it was a great way to have a selection of colors.

When beginning a project, I would search local fabric stores for a wonderful medium- to large-scale print. When I brought the print home, I could pull solids from my collection until I found the perfect mix of colors for my project. The print fabric served as the theme for my project, and the solid colors were selected to match and offset the colors in the print.

I usually don't worry about following color rules in my color selections. I am more interested in contrasts—how a bright yellow will "perk up" the quilt top or if the orange can add "spark" to a dark quilt. In this book I have selected colors that are not my usual style of high bright contrast. It was a fun experience for me to make the project quilts using unfamiliar prints and color combinations. Thanks to the help of the employees at my local quilt shop, we were able to find fabrics for the *Plaid and Stripes* quilt on page 29, which is a style I have never made before. In some of the quilt patterns I limited my selection to just two colors, a real challenge for me! Other projects were made using my new fabric designs, available in quilt and fabric shops as of the initial publication date of this book.

My suggestion is to begin with a color theme and select one fabric that you love and supplement it with ten other fabrics. Most of the patterns in this book require eleven fabrics—two of the fabrics should add a spark or strong contrast.

Since I do not like to measure how much fabric I need for a quilt, I often buy one yard of each color selection. My studio is in a small mountain community, and I cannot run to a fabric store to get more of a particular fabric if needed immediately. I believe when trying a new style, it is best to do small sample quilts. I can always make larger quilts if I know the technique and colors will work for me. Many of the projects in this book are a small size to encourage you to experiment with this new approach to designing quilts by playing with colors and strips.

three

Getting started

Nature's Colors—An Exercise

This exercise is to get you started using the Four-Patch and Nine-Patch blocks, and following my numbering system. Instead of making a quilt I decided to do a mock-up, fused to 1" graph paper. If you don't want to spend a lot on fabrics for this exercise, use colored construction paper which is available at any art supply store. With paper and a glue stick you can practice my technique.

Nature's Colors, 24" x 18", Yvonne Porcella, a mock-up made in fabric on graph paper.

COLOR SELECTION TIPS

Green and brown earth tones dominate the environment where I live but are not commonly used colors in my quilts. My first color selection is a dark green fabric with tiny red dots. To complete a trio of colors in this family, select one medium- and one dark-green small print. A burgundy and a brown with large dark red dots are the next two fabrics that relate to the small red dots in the first fabric. For contrast select two light value fabrics, beige and light brown. The remaining fabrics are one gold print, one sage print, one cheddar print, and one olive green print. Select your eleven colors and rearrange them to test out how they will look in the suggested blocks. Make a chart to follow as you work.

Color Numbering System for Exercise

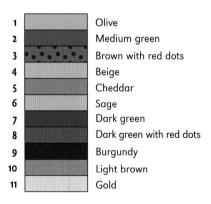

1	Olive
2	Medium green
3	Brown with red dots
4	Beige
5	Cheddar
6	Sage
7	Dark green
8	Dark green with red dots
9	Burgundy
10	Light brown
11	Gold

Fabric Requirements

18" x 22" (fat quarter) of eleven fabrics or 2 pieces of construction paper in each of the 11 colors.

Other Supplies

Glue stick or fusible paper
1" grid graph paper or 1" grid
    Pellon®, 20" x 26"
Scissors or rotary cutter
Cutting mat
12" triangle ruler

NOTE: *The cut strips don't include ¹/₄" seam allowance. If you are going to sew as a quilt, add ¹/₂" to length and width.*

Cutting Strips for Blocks

Chart shows how many strips of each color and width are needed.

Cut all strips across the width of the fabric so they are at least 20" long.

Color Number	Width of Strip to Cut	
	³/₄"	1"
1		2
2		1
3		1
6		1
7		1
8		2
9	1	1
10	1	
11		1

Cutting Strips for the Sashing

For this exercise, cut one ¹/₂", one 1", one 1 ¹/₂", and one 2" strip from each fabric. Cut more strips as you need them. The assembly diagrams that follow will show you the widths of the fabric strips I used, so if you like, you can construct the exercise similar to mine. However, this is a great opportunity to experiment with your fabric strips and blocks.

Make a paste-up of your fabrics for the color numbering system and paste-ups of the Four-Patch and Nine-Patch blocks. (See pages 8-9)

Making the Blocks
Small Four-Patch Blocks
—use ³/₄" wide strips

 Make 5

Large Four-Patch Blocks
—use 1" wide strips

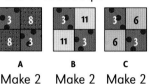

A	B	C
Make 2	Make 2	Make 2

Nine-Patch Blocks
—use 1" wide strips

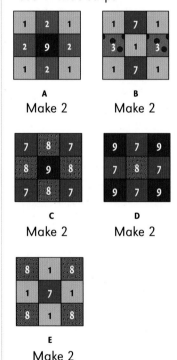

NOTE: *After the blocks are made, mark them with the block letter on a paper note.*

Assembly

Draw 45° diagonal lines on an 18"
x 24" piece of drawing paper using
a 12" triangle ruler.

1.

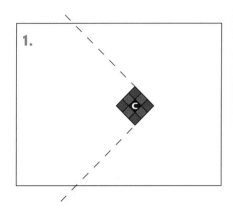

2.

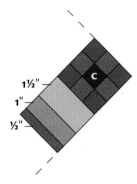

Add strips to make Center Unit.

3.

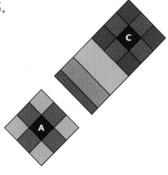

Add a Nine-patch Block A.

4.

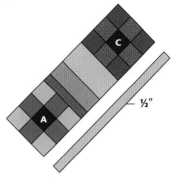

Add strip to one side of Center Unit.

5.

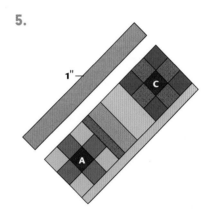

Add strip to opposite side of
Center Unit.

6.

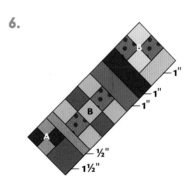

Make Pieced Unit to add to
Center Unit.

7.

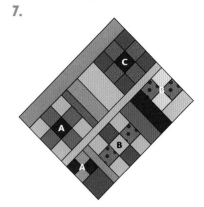

Add Pieced Unit to Center Unit.
Continue adding strips and Pieced
Units as shown in steps 8 through 12.

8.

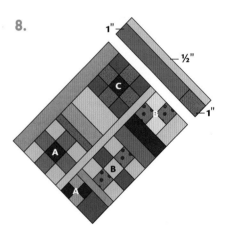

9.

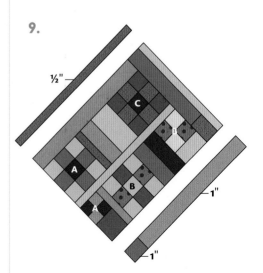

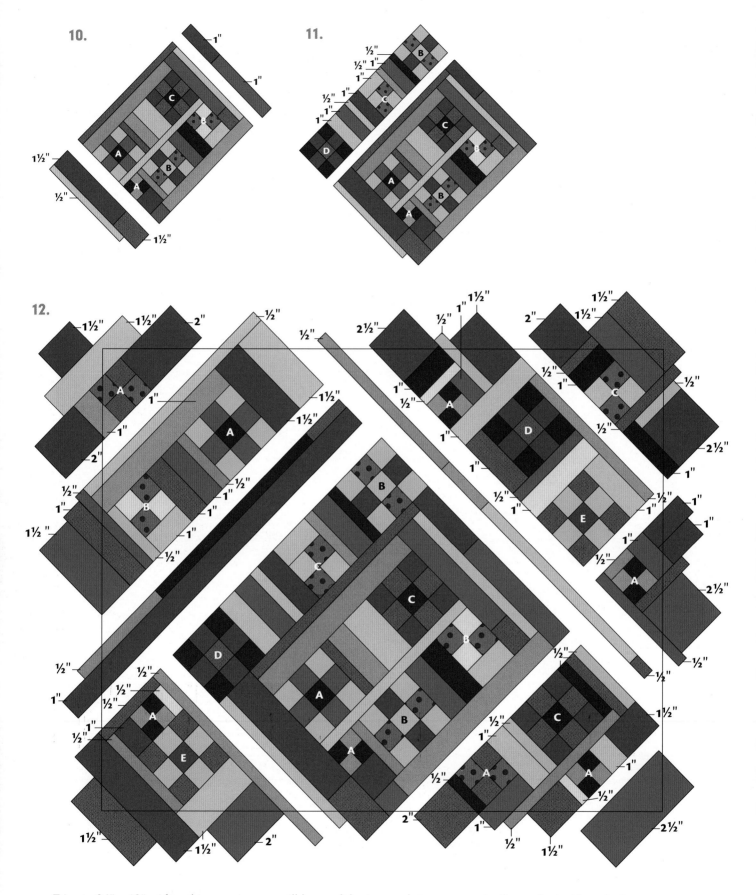

Trim to 24" x 18". After this exercise you will be confident enough to move on to the projects. Have fun!

four

projects

FLIGHT OF FANCY

Bright Contrasts

Flight of Fancy 24" x 18", Yvonne Porcella

Color Selection Tips

The quilt features the complementary colors, red and green, blue and orange, and yellow and purple in a variety of combinations. Select two purples (dark and light), two reds (satin weave and glazed), three greens (turquoise, light green, and green with purple dots), one yellow, one blue, one orange, and one dark pink fabric (from the red family). All the fabric selections form bright contrasts when put together in any combination. The dark purple acts as the dark and the yellow acts as the light. The light green becomes the accent color. When designing the quilt, the placement of these three colors is important for balance.

Color Numbering System

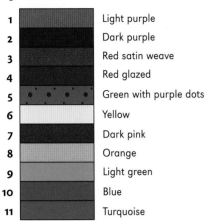

1	Light purple
2	Dark purple
3	Red satin weave
4	Red glazed
5	Green with purple dots
6	Yellow
7	Dark pink
8	Orange
9	Light green
10	Blue
11	Turquoise

Fabric Requirements

²/₃ yard of Fabric 1

18" x 22" (fat quarters) of Fabrics 2-4 and 6-11

2" x 2" square of your selection for Fabric 5

26" x 20" muslin for background

26" x 20" fabric for backing

26" x 20" batting

Cutting Fabric Strips for Blocks and Sashing

Chart shows how many strips of each color and width are needed.

Cut all strips across the width of the fabric so they are at least 20" long.

Color Number	Width of Strip to Cut			
	1"	1 ¹/₂"	2"	3"
1	1	1	5	
2		1	3	
3		1	3	1
4	1		1	1
5	one 2" x 2" square			
6		1	1	
7	1	1	7	
8			4	
9	1	1	3	
10		1		
11			1	

NOTE: *The cut strips include ¹/₄" seam allowance.*

Making the Blocks

Small Four-Patch Blocks
—use 1 ¹/₂" wide strips

A

Make 5

Make a paste-up of your fabrics for the color numbering system and paste-ups of the Four-Patch and Nine-Patch blocks. (See pages 8-9).

Large Four-Patch Blocks—use 2" wide strips

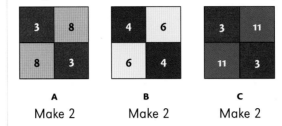

A	B	C
Make 2	Make 2	Make 2

Nine-Patch Blocks—use 2" wide strips

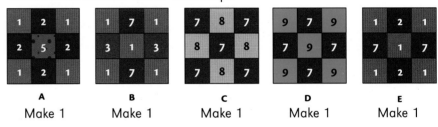

A	B	C	D	E
Make 1	Make 1	Make 1	Make 1	Make 1

NOTE: *After the blocks are made, mark them with the block letter on a paper note.*

Assembly

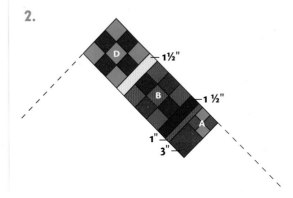

1.

Start with Nine-Patch Block D

2.

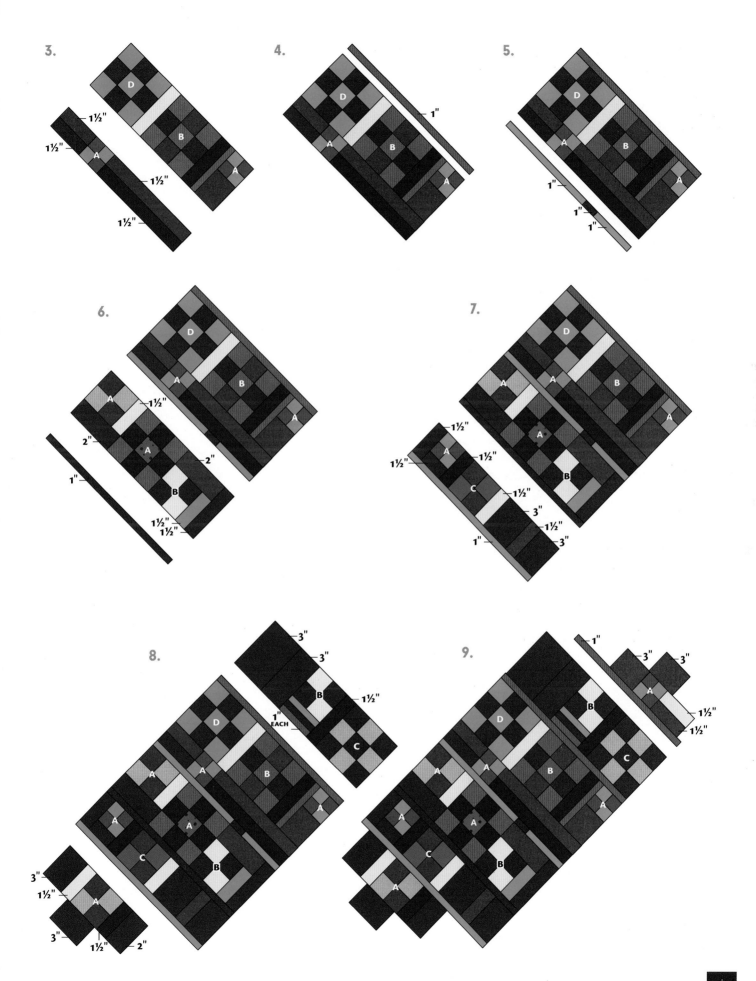

10.

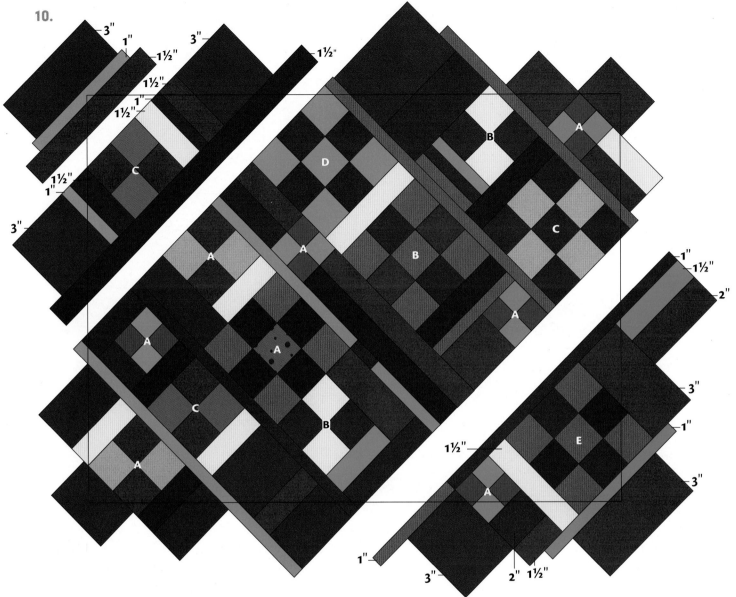

Trim pieced top to 24" x 18". Layer top with batting and backing. Quilt and trim edges even. Bind using Fabric 1.

LANCASTER VIEW

Nine-Patch Variation

Lancaster View, 24" x 20", Yvonne Porcella

Color Selection Tips

Color Numbering System

1		Navy
2		Medium blue
3		Light violet
4		Dark violet
5		Olive
6		Forest
7		Orange
8		Gold
9		Burgundy

Fabric Requirements

3/4 yard of Fabric 1
1/4 yard of Fabrics 2-9
26" x 22" muslin for background
26" x 22" Fabric for backing
26" x 22" batting

Cutting Fabric Strips for Blocks and Sashing

Chart shows how many strips of each color and width are needed.

Cut all strips across the width of the fabric so they are at least 40" long.

Color Number	Width of Strip to Cut			
	1"	1 1/2"	2"	2 1/2"
1	1	3	1	3
2	1	2		
3	1	2		
4		2		
5	1	2		
6		2		
7	1	2		
8		3		
9		4		

Make a paste-up of your fabrics for the color numbering system and paste-ups of the Four-Patch and Nine-Patch blocks. (See pages 8-9).

NOTE: *The cut strips include 1/4" seam allowance.*

The block pattern differs from the others in this book. Here the Nine-Patch is a variation and is made using four Four-Patch blocks that are joined by four strips of the same color and a contrasting color center square. The colored strips and center square form a cross that separates each of the Four-Patch blocks. Two of the Four-Patch blocks are the same color combination.

Only nine colors were used in this quilt. The dominant color is a very dark blue. This dark value makes the bright blocks pop out and the narrow strips of accent colors make the quilt dazzle. This design works best in solid colors. I chose two values of blue, two values of violet, two different greens, one bright orange, one gold, and one burgundy red.

Making the Blocks

Four-Patch Blocks—use 1 1/2" wide strips

A
Make 2

B
Make 4

C
Make 3

D
Make 1

E
Make 3

F
Make 4

G
Make 3

H
Make 3

I
Make 4

J
Make 2

Nine-Patch Blocks

To Make a Nine-Patch A Block:

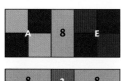

Make 1

To Make a Nine-Patch B Block:

Make 1

To Make a Nine-Patch C Block:

Make 1

To Make a Nine-Patch D Block:

Make 1

NOTE: *Use 1 1/2" wide strips for sashing in the Nine-Patch blocks.*

Assembly

1.

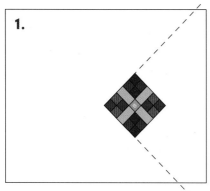

Start with Nine-Patch Block B

2.

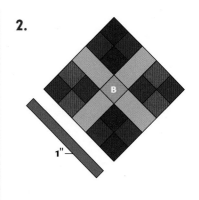

1"

3.

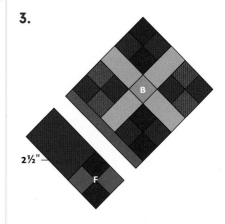

2½"

4.

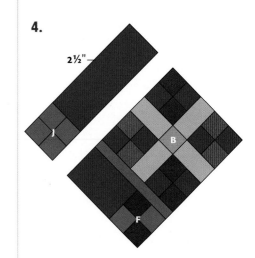

2½"

5.

6.

7.

8.

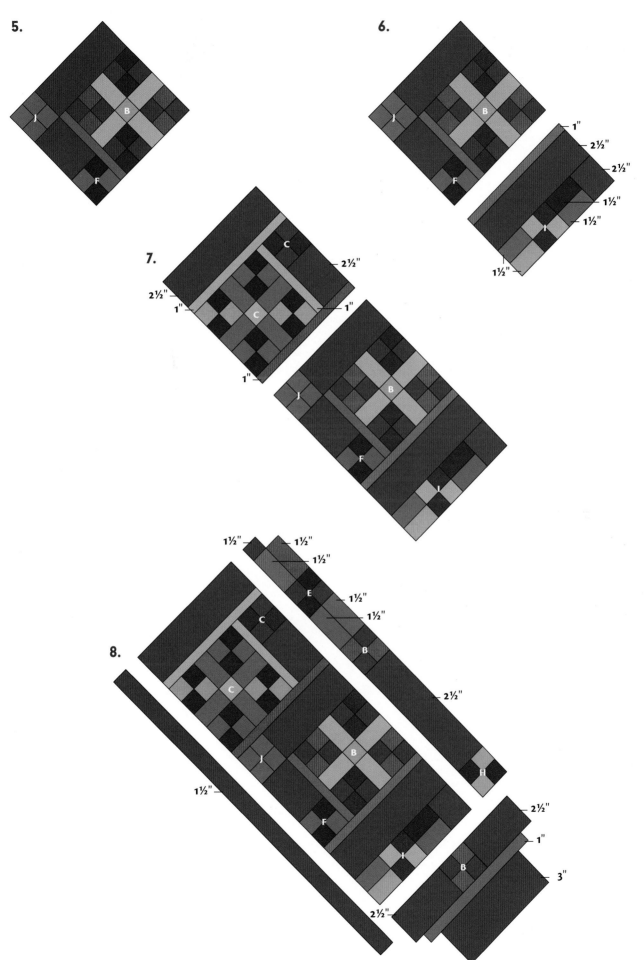

9.

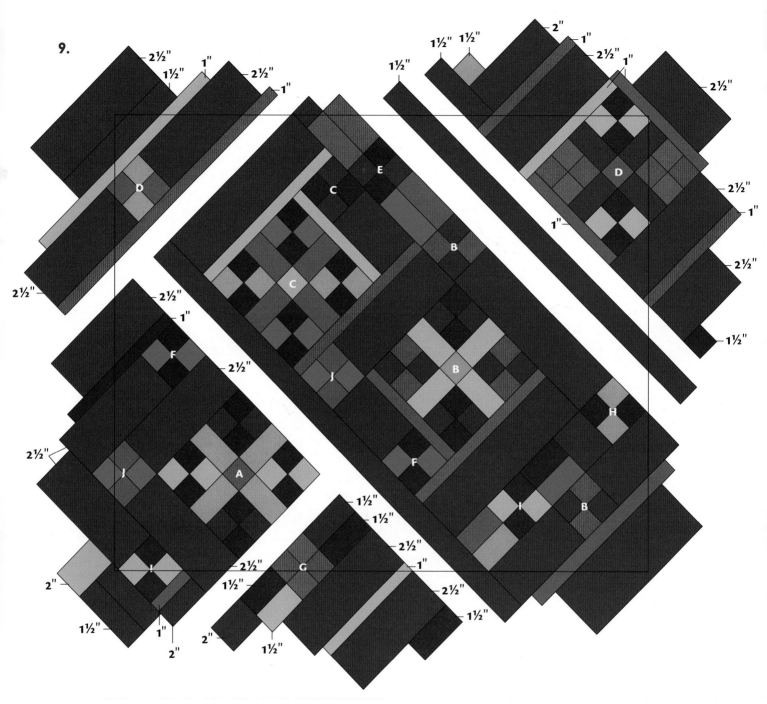

Trim pieced top to 24" x 20". Layer top with batting and backing.
Quilt and trim edges even. Bind using Fabrics 1 and 2.

WINTER'S TALE

Pastel Blues and Gray

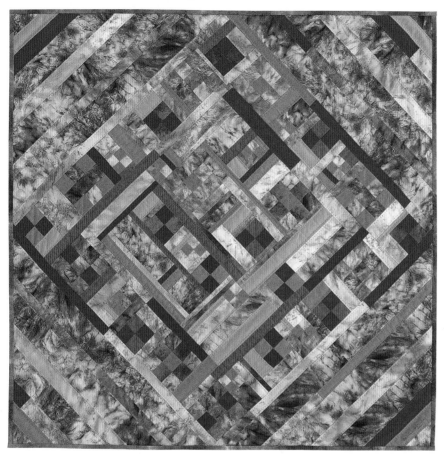

Winter's Tale **45" x 45", hand quilted by Kay Elson and Yvonne Porcella**

Color Selection Tips

As much as I love to work in bright contrast colors, I also appreciate a softer pastel palette.

When designing a line of commercial fabrics I used my watercolor hand-painted fabrics as inspiration. Several of the fabrics dominate this quilt, which reminds me of a foggy January day in Northern California. Surprisingly enough, fog is laden with many colors as the water-charged atmosphere hangs close to the ground. This quilt is a rendering of those colors with hope that the winter's sun will appear and brighten the sky.

The colors selected are close in value but there is high contrast in three of the solid colors. The other fabrics have medium-to-light value within the design, which also works well in strip piecing as each long strip offers many color values.

Color Numbering System

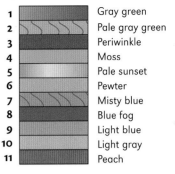

1	Gray green
2	Pale gray green
3	Periwinkle
4	Moss
5	Pale sunset
6	Pewter
7	Misty blue
8	Blue fog
9	Light blue
10	Light gray
11	Peach

Fabric Requirements

$1/2$ yard of each of Fabrics 1-11, except Fabric 7

1 $1/2$ yards of Fabric 7

48" x 48" muslin for background

48" x 48" fabric for backing

48" x 48" batting

Cutting Fabric Strips for Blocks and Sashing Strips

Chart shows how many strips of each color and width are needed.

Cut all strips across the width of the fabric so they are at least 40" long.

Color Number	Width of Strip to Cut			
	1"	1 1/2"	2"	3"
1	1	2	6	
2	1	2	3	
3	1	2	4	
4	1	1		
5	1	2	3	
6		1	2	
7	1	1	5	9
8	1		4	
9	1	2	4	
10	1	1	1	
11	1	1	1	

NOTE: *The cut strips include $1/4$" seam allowance.*

Make a paste-up of your fabrics for the color numbering system and paste-ups of the Four-Patch and Nine-Patch blocks. (See pages 8-9.)

Making the Blocks

Small Four-Patch Blocks—use 1 1/2" wide strips

A

Make 10

Large Four-Patch Blocks—use 2" wide strips

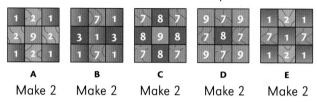

A   **B**   **C**
Make 4   Make 4   Make 4

Nine-Patch Blocks—use 2" wide strips

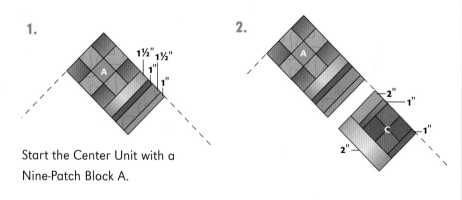

A   **B**   **C**   **D**   **E**
Make 2   Make 2   Make 2   Make 2   Make 2

NOTE: *After the blocks are made, mark them with the block letter on a paper note.*

Assembly

1.

Start the Center Unit with a Nine-Patch Block A.

2.

3.

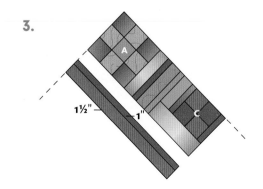

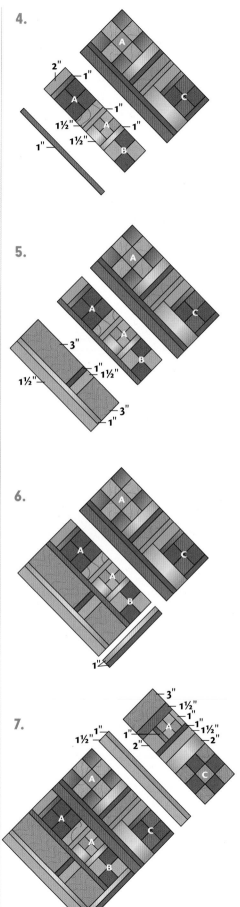

4.

5.

6.

7.

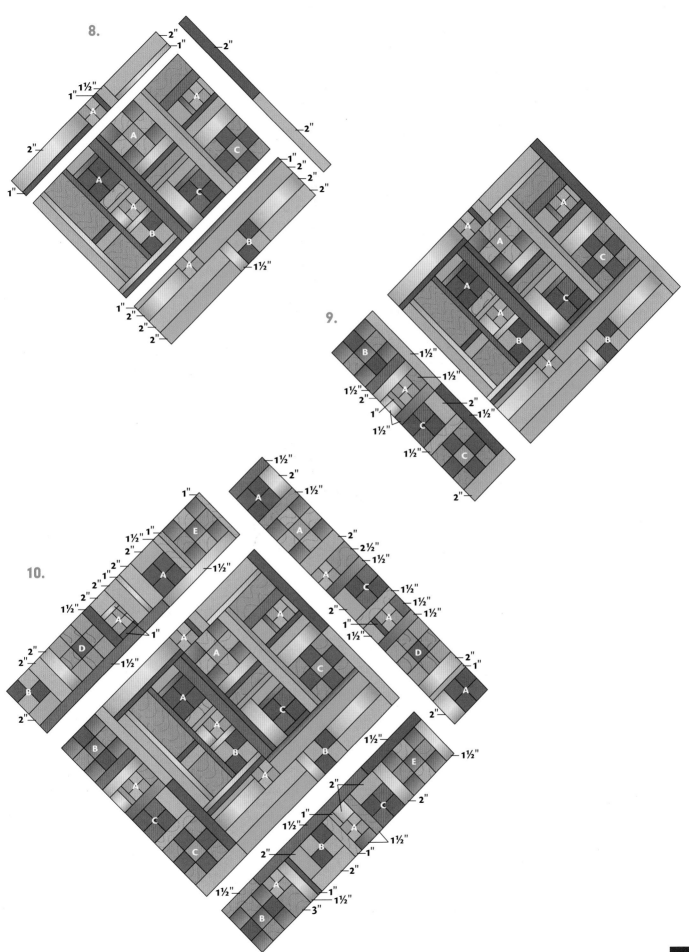

8.

9.

10.

11.

1½" 1½"

1½" 1½"

When you have reached the size want, place the Center Unit on the 48" x 48" foundation fabric to establish the finished quilt size. Add strips needed to finish in all four corners.

Finishing

Trim pieced top to 46" x 46". Layer top with batting and backing. Quilt and trim edges even. Bind using Fabric 8.

12.

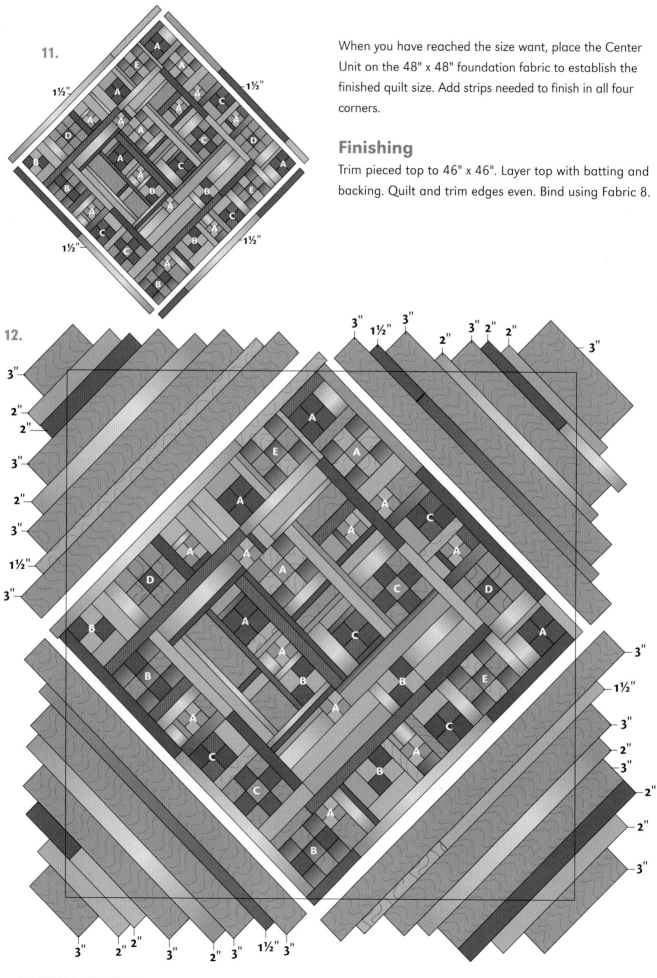

PLAIDS AND STRIPES

Folk Art Style

Plaids and Stripes , 36" x 36", **Yvonne Porcella**

Color Selection Tips

My first fabric selection for this quilt was a brown plaid. Next I found cotton stripe fabrics with a homespun look. This is a woven fabric and the same on the back and front and can be stitched to show either a vertical or horizontal position of the stripe fabric. For this pattern, I chose to use a standard set for the blocks to utilize this variation of the stripe fabrics in my design. I also wanted the quilt to have a well-used look. The plaid fabric had a tendency to stretch when sewn, and I exaggerated upon that by batting this quilt with a woven cotton flannel fabric that also had some stretch. The machine quilting in combination with the woven fabrics and batting enhanced a primitive look to the finished quilt.

To add to the brown plaid I selected an orange print, a brown print, one narrow stripe, two medium stripes, one tan Ikat woven fabric, two blue prints, a dark green, and an olive green print.

Color Numbering System

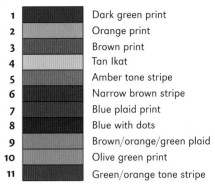

1	Dark green print
2	Orange print
3	Brown print
4	Tan Ikat
5	Amber tone stripe
6	Narrow brown stripe
7	Blue plaid print
8	Blue with dots
9	Brown/orange/green plaid
10	Olive green print
11	Green/orange tone stripe

Fabric Requirements

18" x 22" (fat quarters) of Fabrics
   1, 2, 4 and 10-11
5/8 yard of Fabric 3
1 1/2 yards of Fabric 9
1 1/4 yards cotton for backing
1 1/4 yards cotton flannel 40" wide
   for batting (prewashed)

Cutting Fabric Strips for Blocks and Sashing

Chart shows how many strips of each color and width are needed.

Cut all strips across the fat quarter so they are at least 20" long—except fabrics 3 and 9.

Color	Width of Strip to Cut			
Number	1"	1 1/2"	1 3/4"	2"
1		2	1	5
2		1		7
3		3		8
4		2		5
5	2	1		
6		2		2
7	1	2		2
8	1	1		1
9**		2		7
10		2	1	1
11	2	1		2
**Fabric 9: also cut 4 strips 5 1/2 " x 40"				

NOTE: *The cut strips include 1/4" seam allowance.*

Make a paste-up of your fabrics for the color numbering system and paste-ups of the Four-Patch and Nine-Patch blocks. (See pages 8-9).

Making the Blocks

Small Four-Patch Blocks
—use 1 1/2" wide strips

A
Make 6

Large Four-Patch Blocks
—use 2" wide strips

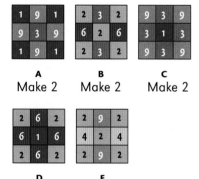

A   **B**   **C**
Make 2   Make 2   Make 2

Nine-Patch Blocks
—use 2" wide strips

A   **B**   **C**
Make 2   Make 2   Make 2

D   **E**
Make 2   Make 1

NOTE: *After the blocks are made, mark them with the block letter on a paper note.*

Assembly

1.

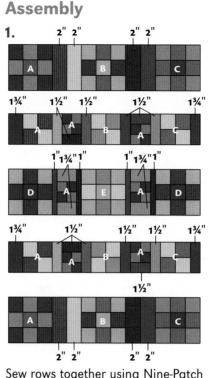

Sew rows together using Nine-Patch blocks and strips.

2.

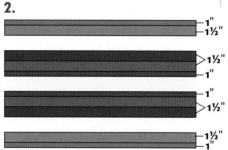

Sew sashing strips.

3.

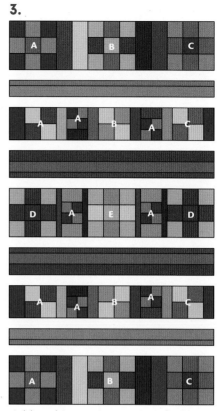

Add sashing strips to pieced rows.

4.

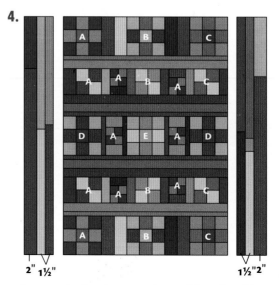

Sew vertical strips together, add to the sides.

5.

5½"

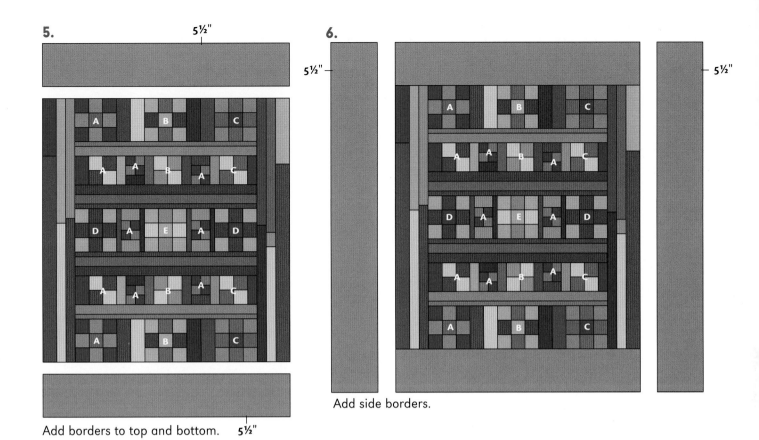

Add borders to top and bottom.   5½"

6.

5½"

5½"

Add side borders.

7.

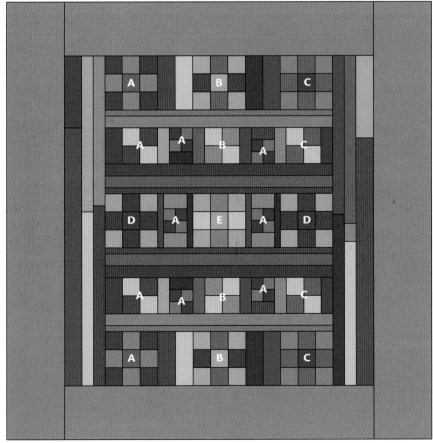

Finished quilt

Finishing

Layer quilt top over prewashed cotton flannel and cotton backing. Quilt and trim edges to 36" x 36". Binding: stitch together all remaining fabrics to use as pieced binding.

SUN AND SKY

Strong Contrast Colors

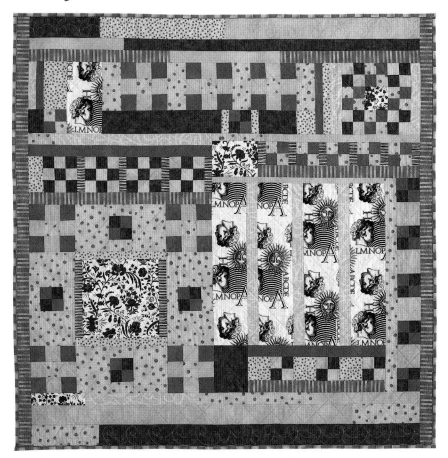

Sun and Sky, 56" x 55", by Yvonne Porcella, machine quilted by Paula Reid

Color Selection Tips

W hat better combination of just two colors than yellow and blue, although this pattern could use many other colors? This quilt is made as a remembrance of a trip I took to the south of France where I purchased a small piece of the blue and white print fabric. My original thought was to make a blue and white quilt, but somehow the yellow just begged to be included. I only had a small piece of the blue and white fabric, and I found the large-scale black and white print in my fabric stash. The pattern is divided up into large rectangle units using Four-and Nine Patch blocks and sashing strips.

The fabric choices are four yellows (two with blue dots, one print, and one solid), two blue fabrics, two specialty prints, one black and white stripe, two blue and yellow prints (a check and a stripe).

Color Numbering System

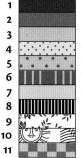

1	Dark blue solid
2	Medium blue solid
3	Yellow solid
4	Yellow with small dots
5	Yellow with large dots
6	Yellow and blue stripe
7	Yellow print
8	Narrow black/white stripe
9	Blue and white print
10	Large-scale black/white print
11	Blue and yellow checks

Fabric Requirements

1 yard each of Fabrics 1, 3, 5, and 10
1/2 yard each of Fabrics 2 and 6
1/4 yard each of Fabrics 4, 7, and 8
18" x 22" of Fabric 9
59" x 58" for backing
59" x 58" batting
1/2 yard of Fabric 11 for binding

Cutting Fabric Strips for Blocks and Sashing

Chart shows how many strips of each color and width are needed.

Cut all strips across the width of the fabric so they are at least 40" long.

Color Number	Width of Strip to Cut				
	1 1/2"	2"	2 1/2"	3"	3 1/2"
1**	2	2	1		2
2	2	2	2		
3	2	4	3	1	1
4	1		1		1
5**	1	2	1	1	1
6		2	4		
7	1	3			
8	1				

**fabric 1: also cut one 5" x 6 1/2" strip

**fabric 5: also cut one 6 1/2" x 40" strip

**fabric 9: cut cut one 10 1/2" x 10 1/2", one 3 1/2" x 3 1/2", one 5 1/2" x 6 1/2", one 2" x 7 1/2"

**fabric 10: cut four 5" x 20 1/2", one 5" x 9 1/2"

**fabric 11: cut six 2 3/4" x 44"

NOTE: *The cut strips include* 1/4" *seam allowance.*

Make a paste-up of your fabrics for the color numbering system and paste-ups of the Four-Patch and Nine-Patch blocks. (See pages 8-9).

Making the Blocks

Four-Patch Blocks

—use 1 1/2" wide strips

A
Make 10

B
Make 7

C
Make 10

Small Nine-Patch Blocks

—use 2" wide strips

A
Make 2

B
Make 2

Large Nine-Patch Blocks

—use 2 1/2" wide strips

A
Make 7

NOTE: *After the blocks are made, mark them with the block letter on a paper note.*

Assembly

1.

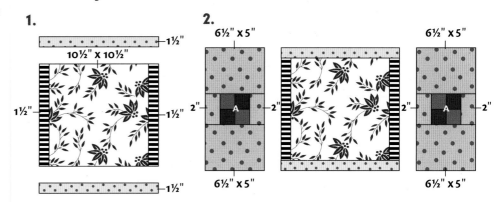

1½"
10½" x 10½"
1½"
1½"
1½"

2.

6½" x 5"
6½" x 5"
2"
2"
6½" x 5"
6½" x 5"

3.

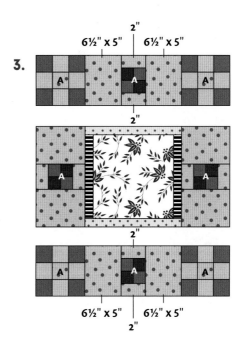

2"
6½" x 5"   6½" x 5"
2"
2"
6½" x 5"   6½" x 5"
2"

4.

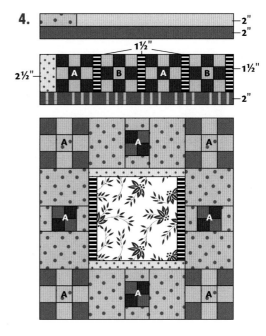

2"
2"
1½"
2½"
A   B   A   B
1½"
2"

5.

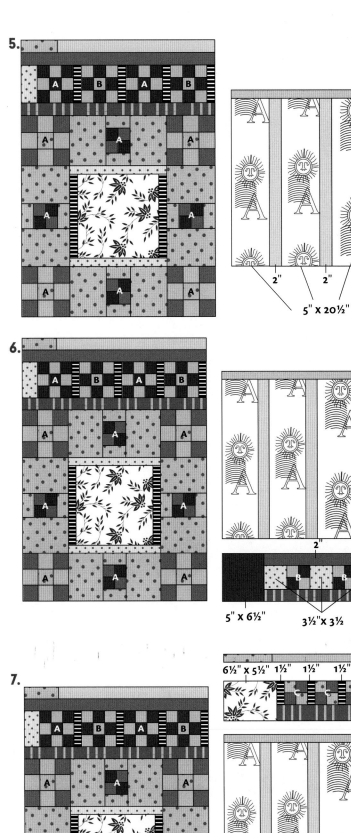

A · B · A · B

A · A · A

A · A

A · A · A

1½"

A · A · A · A

2" · 2" · 2"

5" x 20½"

6.

A · B · A · B

A · A

A · A

A · A · A

2"

A
A
A
A
A

3½"x 3½

2"

A

2"

5" x 6½"

3½"x 3½

B · B · B

7.

A · B · A · B

A · A · A

A · A

A · A · A

6½" x 5½"   1½"   1½"   1½"   1½"   1½"   1½"

1½"

C · C · C

2½"

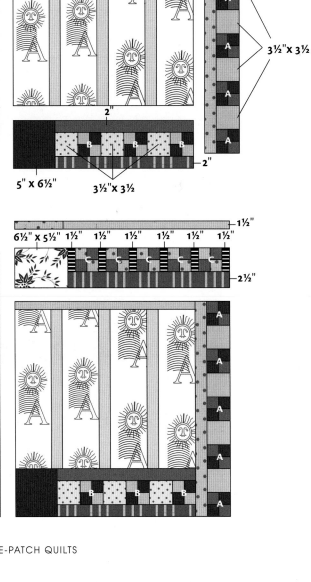

A

A

A

A

B · B

A

8.

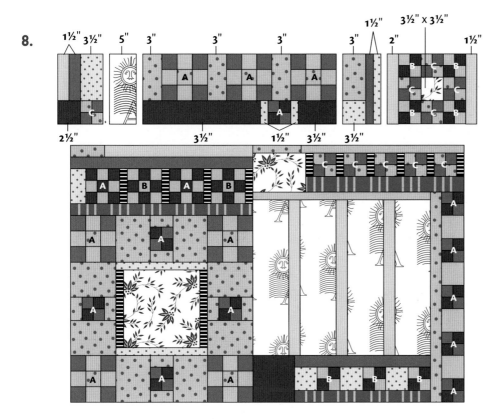

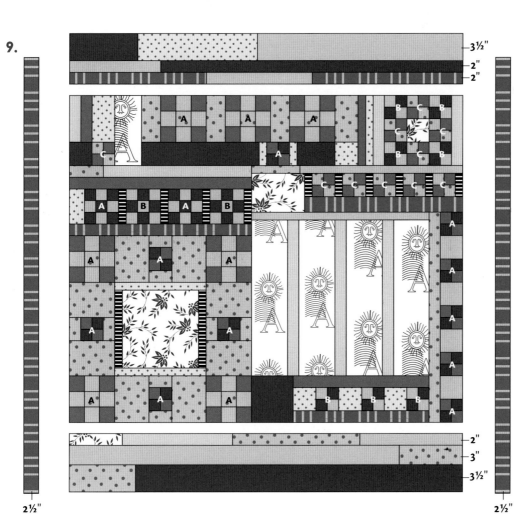

9.

Finishing

Layer top with batting and backing. Quilt, trim edges even. Bind using Fabric 11.

10.

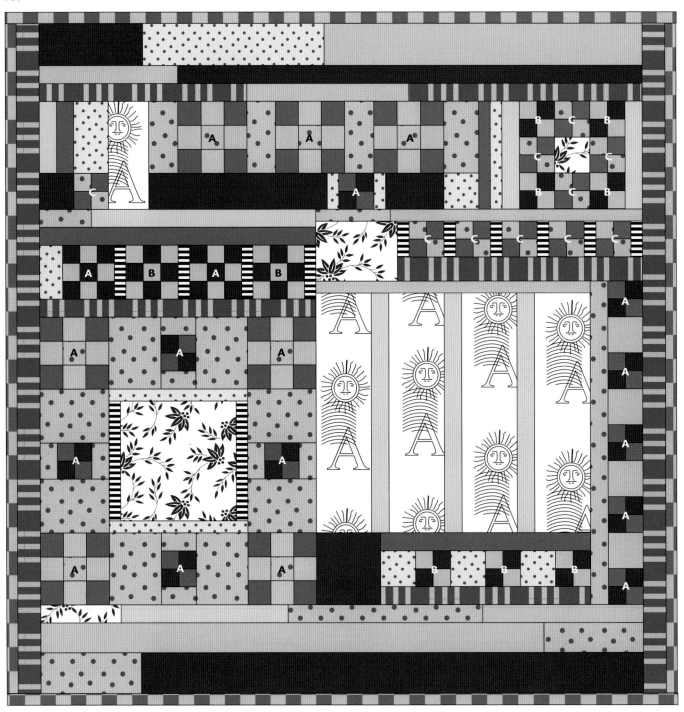

APRON STRINGS

Vintage Reproductions

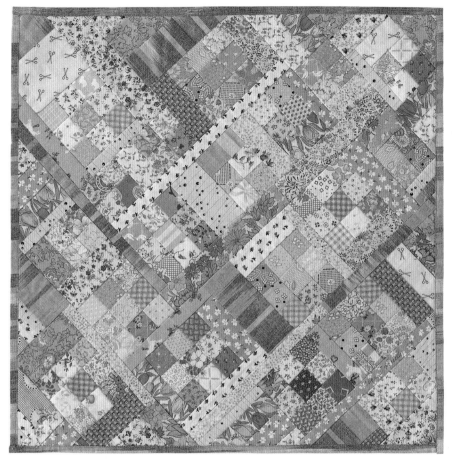

Apron Strings, 18" x 18", Yvonne Porcella, Four-Patch and Nine-Patch blocks made by Judy Mullen

Color Selection Tips

Vintage 1930s fabric prints were reproduced in the late twentieth century, and quilters embraced the soft palette and variety of motifs to make quilts reflective of earlier style quilts. In 1992 Judy Mullen made the blocks using vintage fabrics she had collected most faithfully over the years. My goal was to use her vintage prints for the blocks and pull fabrics from my collection of 1970s-1990s vintage fabrics to use for the sashing strips. This small quilt is a scrap, or charm quilt. Over a 140 different prints were used for the Four-Patch blocks, the Nine-Patch blocks, and for the sashing. Only a few fabrics have been repeated in the blocks. The close value range of these pale-toned prints gives it a soft look. Notice how the lighter value colors are combined with darker-value colors in each block. In some cases the contrast appears in the combining of two different colors, such as green prints and yellow prints, and in others the scale of print forms the contrast.

NOTE: *Rather than using batting, this quilt was foundation pieced to the background fabric.*

Color Numbering System

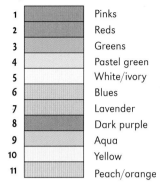

1		Pinks
2		Reds
3		Greens
4		Pastel green
5		White/ivory
6		Blues
7		Lavender
8		Dark purple
9		Aqua
10		Yellow
11		Peach/orange

You will need about 140 assorted prints from the following color groups. Vary your choices in the scale of the prints as well as in color combinations.

Fabric Requirements

Only a small amount of each fabric is needed, most strips are cut 1 1/2" or less. You will need a few 2" pieces. Try to collect as wide a range of fabrics as possible to give this quilt the spirit of the 1930s! Consider doing a fabric swap with your quilt guild.

20" x 20" muslin for background (prewashed)
19" x 19" fabric for backing
20" x 20" batting (optional)
1/4 yard for binding

Make a paste-up of your fabrics for the color numbering system and paste-ups of the Four-Patch and Nine-Patch blocks. (See pages 8-9).

NOTE: *All strips include 1/4" seam allowance.*

Cutting Fabric Strips for Blocks and Sashing

Cut fabric for blocks into 1 1/2" wide strips. Cut fabrics for sashing in 1", 1 1/2", 2" widths. You may need a few wider strips of selected fabrics. Cut all strips 40" long.

Making the Blocks

Large Four-Patch Blocks—use 1 1/2" wide strips

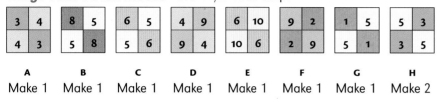

A	B	C	D	E	F	G	H
Make 1	Make 1	Make 1	Make 1	Make 1	Make 1	Make 1	Make 2

Nine-Patch Blocks—use 1 1/2" wide strips

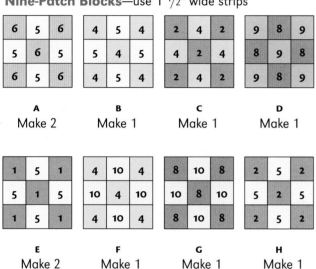

A	B	C	D
Make 2	Make 1	Make 1	Make 1

E	F	G	H
Make 2	Make 1	Make 1	Make 1

NOTE: *After the blocks are made, mark them with the block letter on a paper note.*

Assembly

This quilt was made using single sashing strips between blocks. Notice that the sashing strips are sometimes two prints pieced together, which further blurs the boundaries of the blocks.

Flip and Stitch

This quilt was pieced directly onto a foundation. This method is explained in General Instructions, page 12.

Assembly

1.

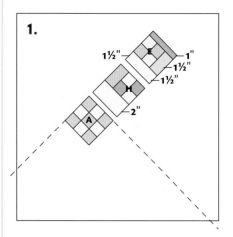

2.

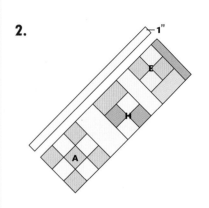

3.

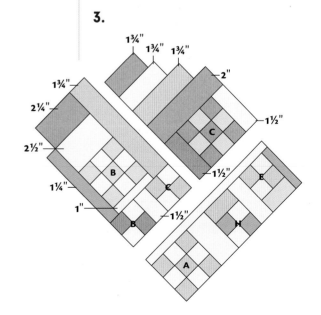

9.

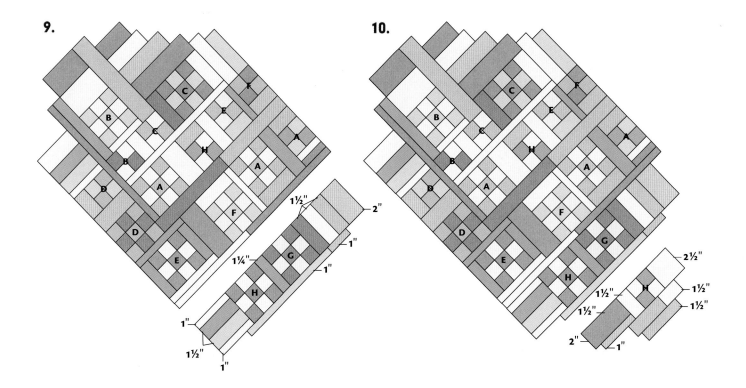

10.

11.

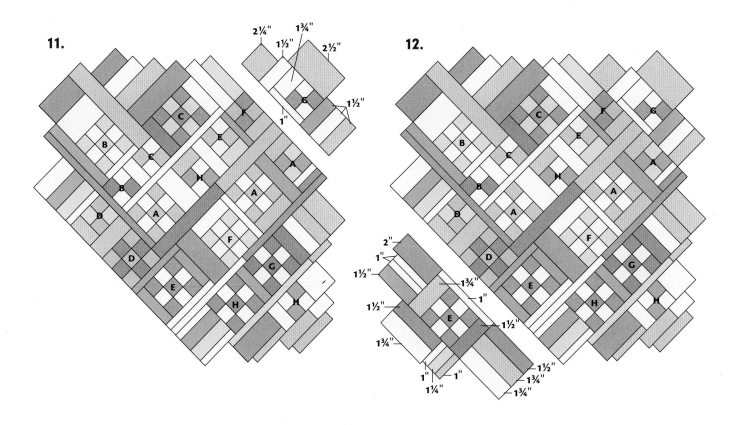

12.

Finishing

Trim the patchwork and foundation to 18 $\frac{1}{2}$" x 18 $\frac{1}{2}$". Layer a 19" x 19" square of your backing fabric wrong sides together behind the foundation (quilt top). Instead of using binding strips, fold the top and bottom edges of the backing $\frac{1}{4}$", then fold again over the edge of the patchwork; pin, machine, or hand stitch in place. Fold $\frac{1}{4}$" at the two sides of the backing, fold again over the edge of the patchwork, and tuck in the outside raw edges, pin, machine or hand stitch in place.

13.

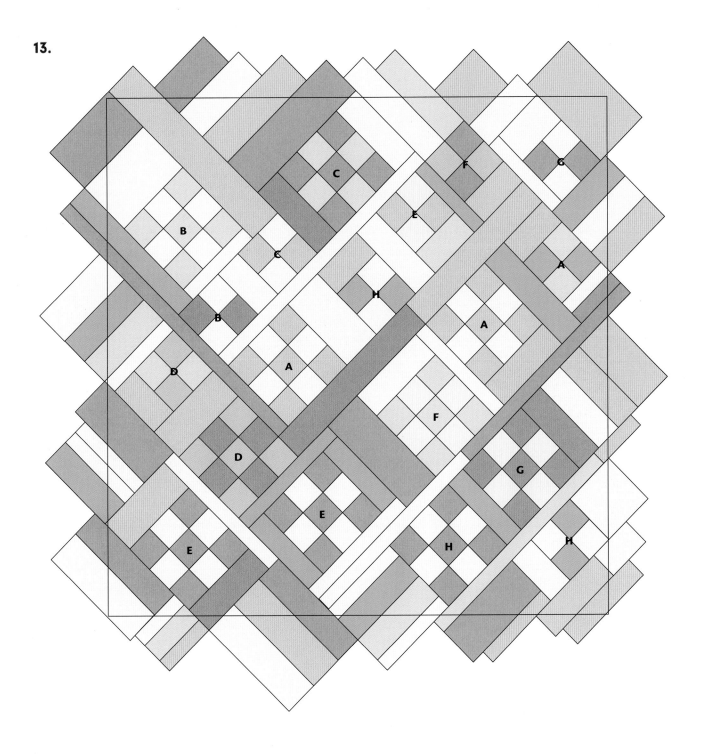

DECEMBER MEMORIES

Holiday Colors

December Memories, 37" x 37", Yvonne Porcella

Color Selection Tips

Decemember is the month associated with traditional complementary colors of red and green. It is difficult to imagine that these two colors when mixed together as pure pigments in equal parts yield a neutral color called brown. Here we can sing the praises of pure red and pure green to make a very traditional holiday theme quilt. It is constructed using the standard set, balanced design so that it may be viewed from any side or on point.

Using just two colors is very limiting, but within the family of reds there are many choices, as well as in the green family. Personally, I love the contrast of a great bright red color next to a clear green. I selected five greens and six reds with three of the fabrics over printed with gold designs, one red and green print, and one mottled green with yellow dots. The remaining six fabrics are prints that have areas of light and dark.

Color Numbering System

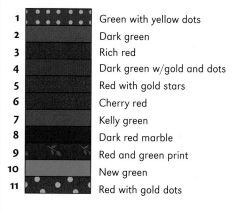

1	Green with yellow dots
2	Dark green
3	Rich red
4	Dark green w/gold and dots
5	Red with gold stars
6	Cherry red
7	Kelly green
8	Dark red marble
9	Red and green print
10	New green
11	Red with gold dots

Fabric Requirements

18" x 22" (fat quarters) of Fabrics 1, 2, 4, 5 and 8

1/4 yard each of Fabrics 3 and 9

1/2 yard each of Fabrics 6, 7, 10 and 11

39" x 39" muslin for background

39" x 39" backing fabric

39" x 39" batting

1/3 yard binding red and green striped fabric

Cutting Fabric Strips for Blocks and Sashing

Fabric 1: cut six 1 1/2" x 22"

Fabric 2: cut five 1 1/2" x 22"

Fabric 3: cut one 1 1/2" x 40", two 2" X 40"

Fabric 4: cut one 2" x 22"

Fabric 5: cut one 2" x 22"

Fabric 6: cut four 1 1/2" x 40", three 2" X 40"

Fabric 7: cut four 1 1/2" x 1 1/2" squares, two 1" x 40", three 2" x 40

Fabric 8: cut four 2" x 22"

Fabric 9: cut four 1 1/2" x 40"

Fabric 10: cut six 1 1/2" x 40"

Fabric 11: cut four 3" x 40"

NOTE: *The cut strips include $1/4"$ seam allowance.*

Make a paste-up of your fabrics for the color numbering system and paste-ups of the Four-Patch and Nine-Patch blocks. (See pages 8-9).

Making the Blocks

Four-Patch Blocks
—use 2" wide strips

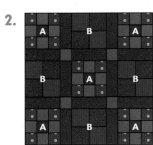

3 8	4 5	6 7
8 3	5 4	7 6
A	**B**	**C**
Make 16	Make 4	Make 24

Nine-Patch Blocks
—use 1 1/2" wide strips

| 1 2 1 |
| 2 3 2 |
| 1 2 1 |
| **A** |
| Make 21 |

NOTE: *After the blocks are made, mark them with the block letter on a paper note.*

Assembly

1.

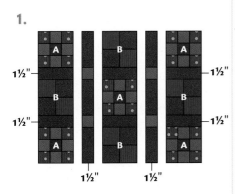

1½"   1½"

1½"   1½"

1½"   1½"

2.

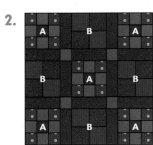

Center Unit

3.

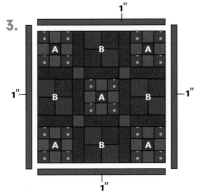

1"   1"

1"   1"

1"

Add sashing to sides of Center Unit.

4.

Make 4 Four-Patch A Sashing Rows.

5.

Add Nine-Patch A to Four-Patch Sashing Rows.

6.

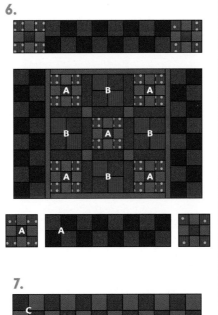

7.

Make four Four-Patch C Sashing Rows.

8.

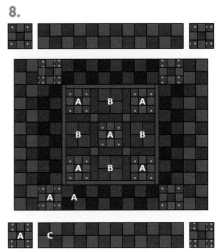

Add Nine-Patch A to Four-Patch C Sashing Rows.

9.

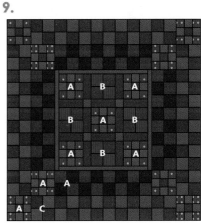

Add Four-Patch C Sashing Rows with Nine-Patch A Corner Blocks.

10.

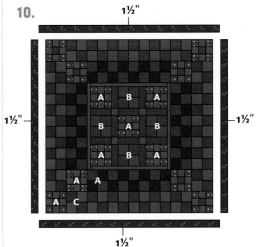

1½"   1½"

1½"   1½"

1½"

Sew sashing to Center Unit.

11.

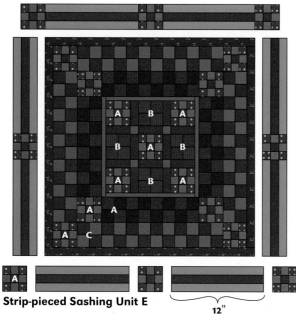

Strip-pieced Sashing Unit E

12"

Using Fabrics 6 and 10, sew three 1 1/2" x 40" strips together to make Sashing Unit E. Cut 8 sections about 12" (measure to be sure). To make the complete sashing, piece a Nine-Patch A in the center of each sashing strip. Add a Nine-Patch A to all four corners. Add outer border using 3" wide strips.

Finishing

Layer pieced top over batting and backing. Quilt and trim edges to 37" x 37". Bind using striped fabric.

12.

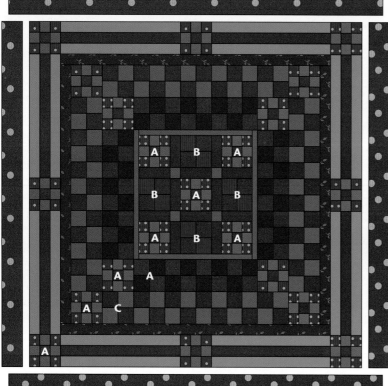

Two Guest Artists

Nancy Podolsky and **Cathie Hoove**r have each contributed a quilt made using the Magical Four-Patch and Nine-Patch system. Both quilters used the general instructions and created different and interesting quilts. Look carefully at the placement of their Four-Patch and Nine-Patch blocks, strips as sashing, borders. Once you understand the concept of a select number of colors, and a limited number of blocks and strips to join them together, it is easy to "read" their quilts. Both artists used a diagonal set. Nancy added three borders to the center-pieced unit and Cathie omitted borders.

Color Selection Tips

Nancy chose a vibrant floral fabric as her inspiration to select fabrics for the quilt blocks and strips. She picked out small print fabrics to match specific colors found in the large floral.

Nancy's choices include light and dark blues, dark purple, black, light and medium green, four rose prints, medium purple for binding and the large floral fabric as strips to accent the colors in the quilt. She used fourteen small Four-Patch, fifteen large Four-Patch, and eight Nine-Patch blocks. Three blocks have been trimmed to fit the diagonal set at the edge before the first border row. She also sewed her small and large Four-Patch blocks together to make either a pieced strip or a square block.

Nancy's Quilt, 42 1/2" x 43 1/2", **Nancy Podolsky**

CATHIE'S QUILT

Color Selection Tips

Cathie selected two very large print fabrics and accented these with other prints in strong colors and patterns. It is a bit more difficult to define her blocks among the bright colors.

Cathie's choices were two black and white prints, three pinks, one red with dots, one raspberry, one stripe, one large floral print, one yellow stripe, and one sunset print. Cathie used five small Four-Patch blocks, ten large Four-Patch blocks, and five Nine-Patch blocks. Some of her large Four-Patch blocks are stitched to make a pieced strip and trimmed on the outside edge.

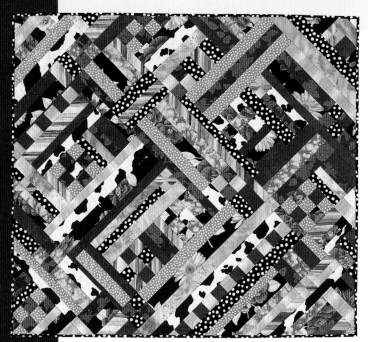

Cathie's Quilt , 39 1/2" x 36 1/2", **Cathie I. Hoover**

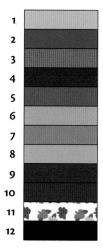

Color Numbering System

1. Light blue
2. Medium green
3. Rose
4. Orange
5. Medium blue
6. Gold with dots
7. Light orange
8. Light green
9. Purple
10. Dark Blue
11. Print with rose, gold, and blue
12. Black

Fabric Requirements

¹/₂ to 1 yard of Fabrics 1-12 depending on fabrics selected for borders.

³/₈ yard fabric for binding

45" x 46" muslin for background

45" x 46" fabric for backing

45" x 46" batting

Making the Blocks

Small Four-Patch Blocks—use 1" wide strips

A
Make 14

Large Four-Patch Blocks—use 2" wide strips

A   **B**   **C**
Make 6   Make 5   Make 4

Nine-Patch Blocks—use 2" wide strips

A   **B**   **C**   **D**   **E**
Make 2   Make 2   Make 2   Make 1   Make 1

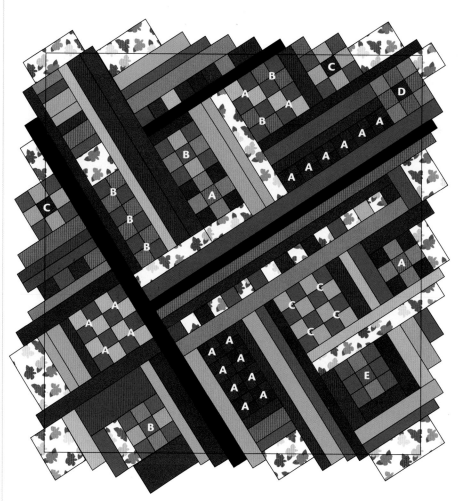

Color Numbering System

1. Pink with white dots
2. Raspberry
3. Pale pink
4. Black with white dots
5. Diagonal stripes
6. Large black and white floral print
7. Black and white large print
8. Rose print
9. Red with purple dots
10. Yellow stripe
11. Sunset

Fabric Requirements

$1/2$ to 1 yard of Fabrics 1-11
$3/8$ yard fabric for binding
41" x 39" muslin for background
41" x 39" fabric for backing
41" x 39" batting

Making the Blocks

Small Four-Patch Blocks—use 1" wide strips

A
Make 5

Large Four-Patch Blocks—use 2" wide strips

A   **B**   **C**   **D**

Make 2   Make 2   Make 2   Make 4

Nine-Patch Blocks—use 2" wide strips

A   **B**   **C**   **D**   **E**

Make 1   Make 1   Make 1   Make 1   Make 1

About the Author

Elaine F. Keenan, photographer

Yvonne Porcella has been working as a fiber artist since the early 1960s. In addition to hand-woven garments, she also produced patchwork garments and had her first gallery exhibition in 1972. Many of her works have been acquired by museums across the United States and she recently gifted her extensive collection of ethnic fabrics and costumes to the San Jose (California) Museum of Quilts and Textiles.

Through her teaching, lectures, appearances, and exhibitions, Yvonne is a major influence in the fields of quilting and wearable art. Her work has been showcased in the book *Yvonne Porcella, Art and Inspirations* and she has also written other books about quilting and surface design.

She has been honored by her peers with induction into the Quilters Hall of Fame and has been awarded the Silver Star by the International Quilt Association. She is a founding member of the Studio Art Quilt Associates and until recently served as the President of the Board of Directors.

Yvonne resides in Northern California with her husband and enjoys her lively family that includes eleven grandchildren.

Other Books by Yvonne Porcella

Other Fine Books From C&T Pulishing

Block Magic: Over 50 Fun & Easy Blocks made from Squares and Rectangles, Nancy Johnson-Srebro

Color Play: Easy Steps to Imaginative Color in Quilts, Joen Wolfrom

Crazy Quilt Handbook, 2nd Edition, Judith Montano

Cut-Loose Quilts: Stack, Slice, Switch & Sew, Jan Mullen

Fantastic Fabric Folding: Innovative Quilting Projects, Rebecca Wat

Freddy's House: Brilliant Color in Quilts, Freddy Moran

Hand Appliqué with Alex Anderson: Seven Projects for Hand Appliqué, Alex Anderson

In the Nursery: Creative Quilts and Designer Touches, Jennifer Sampou & Carolyn Schmitz

Kaleidoscopes: Wonders of Wonder, Cozy Baker

Kaleidoscopes & Quilts, Paula Nadelstern

Laurel Burch Quilts: Kindred Creatures, Laurel Burch

Lone Star Quilts and Beyond: Projects and Inspiration, Jan Krentz

Machine Embroidery and More: Ten Step-by-Step Projects Using Border Fabrics & Beads, Kristen Dibbs

Pieced Flowers, Ruth B. McDowell

Piecing: Expanding the Basics, Ruth B. McDowell

Quilt It for Kids: 11 Projects, Sports, Fantasy & Animal Themes, Quilts for Children of All Ages, Pam Bono

Quilted Memories: Celebrations of Life, Mary Lou Weidman

The Quilted Garden: Design & Make Nature-Inspired Quilts, Jane A. Sassaman

Quilting with the Muppets: The Jim Henson Company in Association with Sesame Workshop

Quilts, Quilts, and More Quilts! Diana McClun and Laura Nownes

Rx for Quilters: Stitcher-Friendly Advice for Every Body, Susan Delaney Mech, M.D.

Setting Solutions, Sharyn Craig

Shadow Redwork™ with Alex Anderson: 24 Designs to Mix and Match, Alex Anderson

Strips 'n Curves: A New Spin on Strip Piecing, Louisa Smith

Two-for-One Foundation Piecing: Reversible Quilts and More, Wendy Hill

For more information write for a free catalog:
C&T Publishing, Inc.
P.O. Box 1456
Lafayette, CA 94549
(800) 284-1114
e-mail: ctinfo@ctpub.com
website: www.ctpub.com

For quilting supplies:
Cotton Patch Mail Order
3405 Hall Lane, Dept. CTB
Lafayette, CA 94549
(800) 835-4418
(925) 283-7883
e-mail: quiltusa@yahoo.com
website: www.quiltusa.com